The Barack & Michelle Obama

Paper Doll
&
Cut-Out Book

JOHN BOSWELL

ILLUSTRATIONS BY RANDY JONES
&
SUSANN FERRIS JONES

St. Martin's Griffin
New York

THE BARACK & MICHELLE OBAMA PAPER DOLL & CUT-OUT BOOK.
Copyright © 2009 by John Boswell Management Inc. All rights reserved. Printed in Peru. For information, address St. Martin's Press, 175 Fifth Avenue, New York, N.Y. 10010.

www.stmartins.com

ISBN-13: 978-0-312-60050-1
ISBN-10: 0-312-60050-X

First Edition: June 2009

10 9 8 7 6 5 4 3 2 1

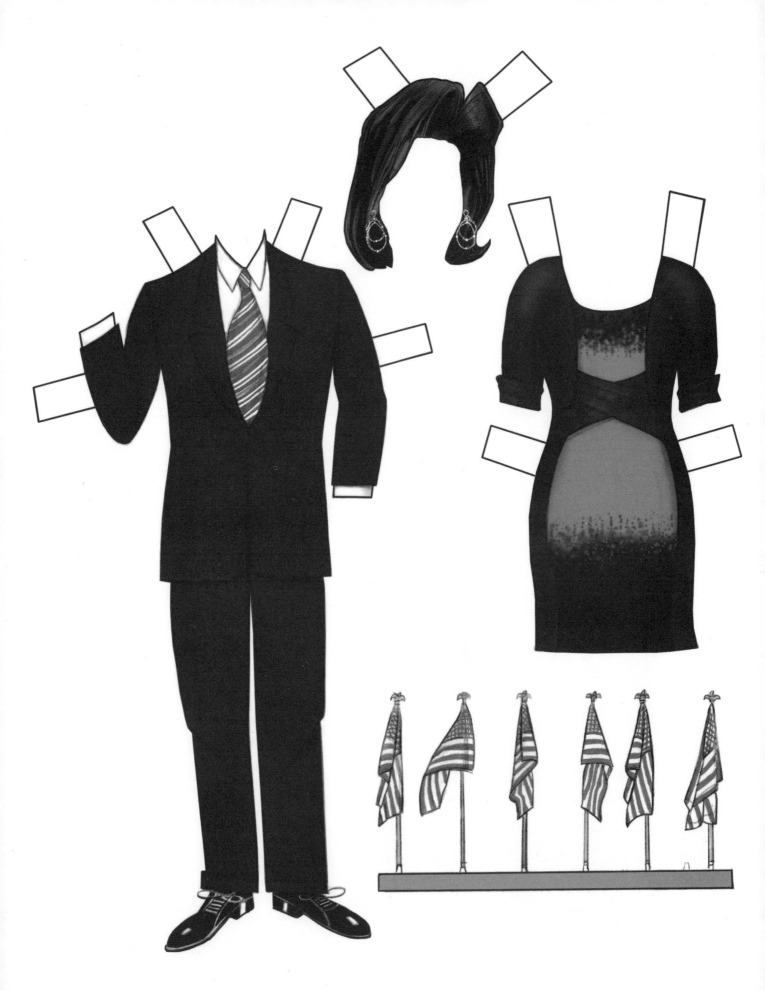

ELECTION NIGHT

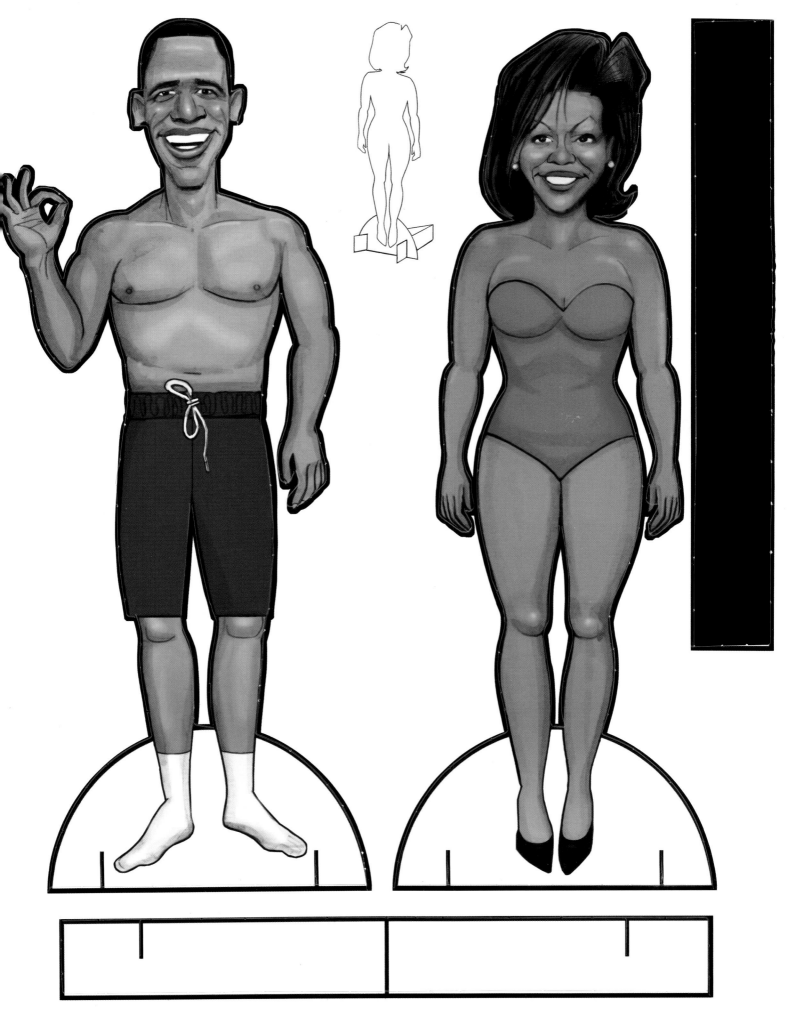

INAUGURATION DAY

THE INAUGURAL BALLS

FIRST DAY OF WORK

DAY OF SERVICE

THE ATHLETE

MICHELLE'S CLOSET

MICHELLE'S CLOSET

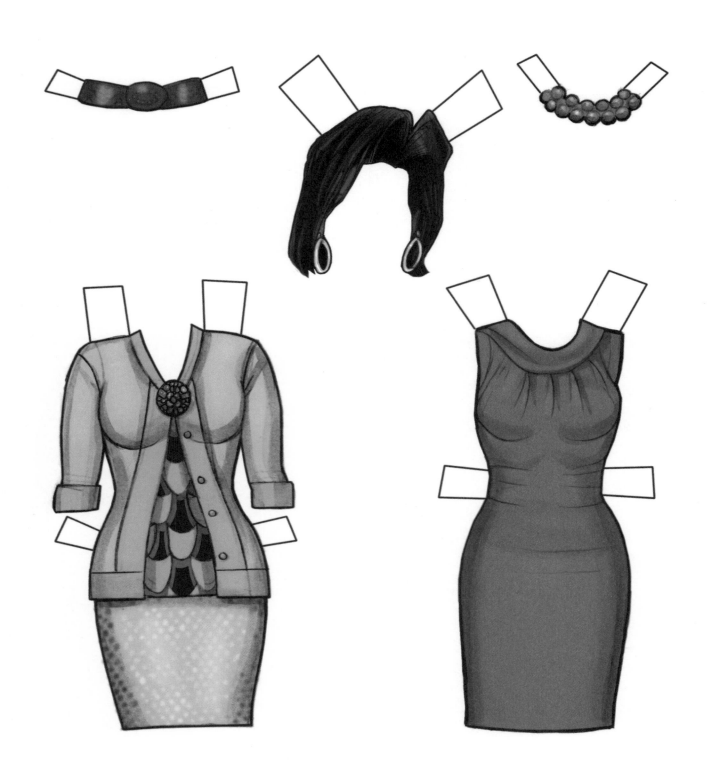

MICHELLE'S CLOSET

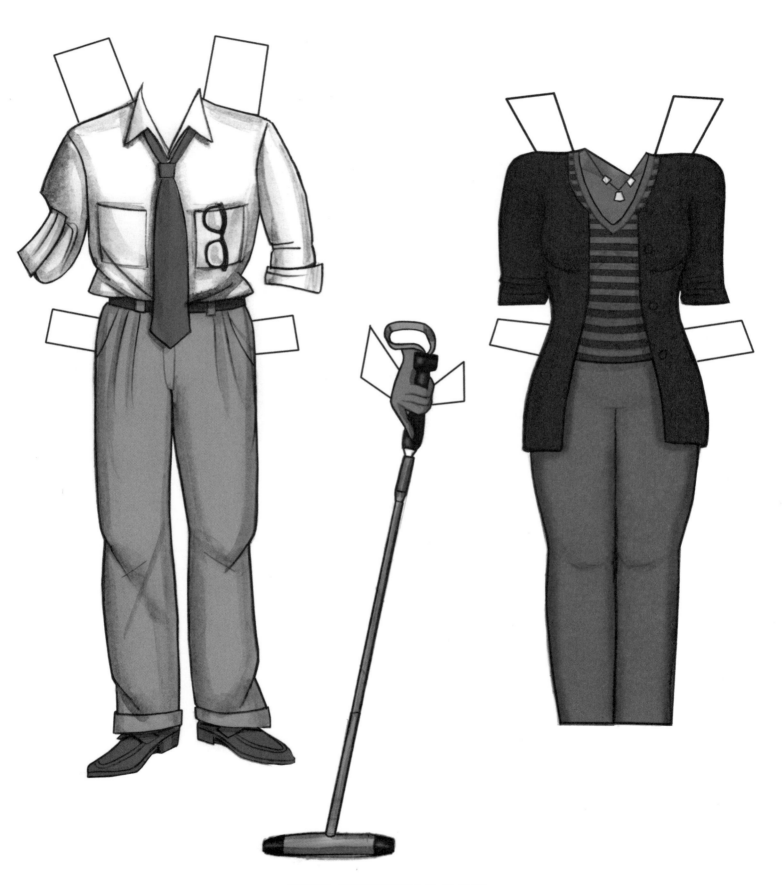

THE PREPPY LOOK

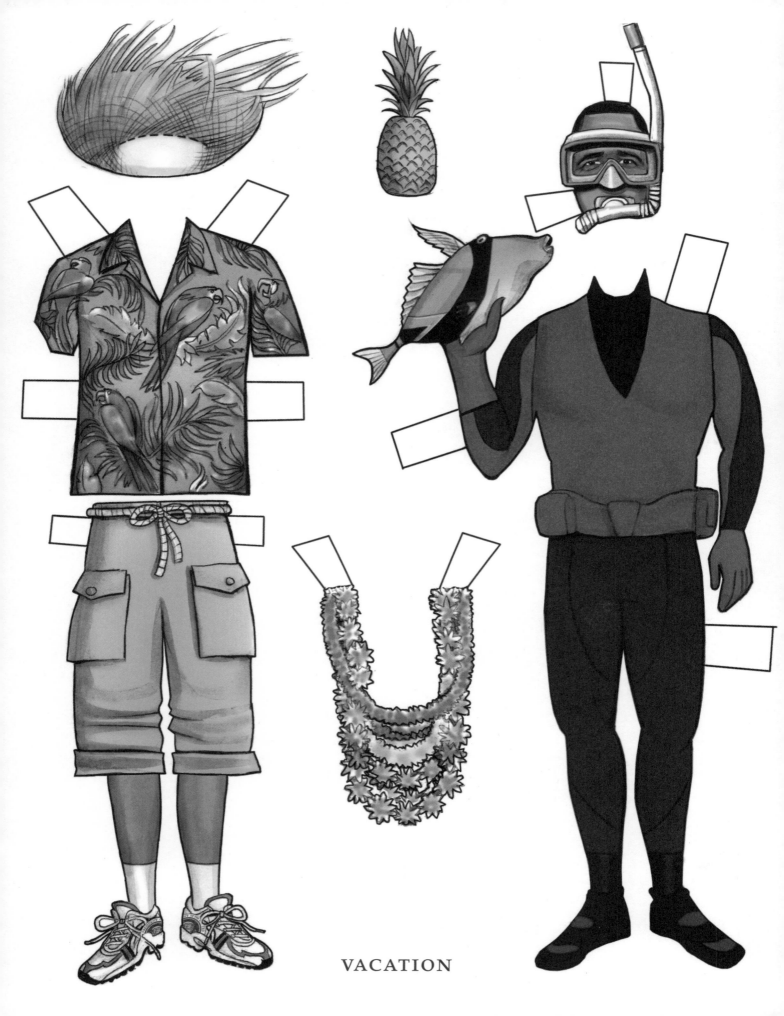

VACATION

VACATION

FOREIGN AFFAIRS
KENYA

FOREIGN AFFAIRS
RUSSIA

CAMP DAVID